ILLUSORY

SIX THINGS MENTALLY-FREE PEOPLE DON'T BELIEVE, WHICH STRESSED AND ANXIOUS PEOPLE DO

ALEX MATHERS

MIND LADDER PRESS

All Rights Reserved.

Alex Mathers, 2020

Mind Ladder Press

1st Edition

Illustrations and cover design by the author.

No part of this book may be reproduced or transmitted in any form without the written permission of the author, except for the inclusion of brief quotations in a review.

If you believe this copy was sold to you through an illegitimate source, please notify the author with details of where you got this by contacting alex@alexmathers.net.

ALSO BY ALEX MATHERS

Promo 3.0

How to Get Illustration Clients

The Indispensable Illustrator

Joining the Dots

The Five Secret Truths

PRAISE FOR ALEX'S OTHER BOOKS

'Joining the Dots:'

"Brilliantly useful, as tends to be the case with Alex Mathers output - be it in book format, or on his blog. As a creative, I've been reading his writings for a number of years, and they serve to educate, share, and uplift in equal measures." — LittlePurpleGoth, Amazon Reviewer

"As some one who has worked for themselves in the creative arena a few years back, I wish this book had been available to read back then. Its inspirational and informative and honest." — Karen, Amazon Reviewer

'How to Get Illustration Clients:'

"This is a fantastic guide and essential to anyone working as a freelancer." — Philip Dennis

"I'm not an illustrator myself, but still found all the principles in the book really useful. This book is clear, concise, and full of good info. Alex's approach is ethical and authentic, and he's really into building sustainable business." — Dave Rock

'The Indispensable Illustrator:'

"With the Indispensable Illustrator, Mathers continues to establish himself a clear, concise and knowledgeable voice amongst the shelves of generic marketing guides." — Michael Cunliffe

"Aimed specifically at illustrators but easily applicable to any creative profession. It's refreshing to see a book cover the matters that aren't taught in courses or most people struggle with, such as confidence and self-worth. Already I've felt a boost to my own work and mindset and I can see this being my 'yearly self review' bible." — Amy, Amazon Reviewer

FREE BONUS BOOK:

'The Five Secret Truths:

Uncover your confidence, work with your fear, and be unstoppable.'

Learn the 'Five Secret Truths' that helped Alex overcome anxiety, see hidden opportunities, tap into boundless creativity and energy, and create a tremendous 'unfair advantage' in his life.

Follow these steps right now to grab your free booklet copy before it's gone:

- Head to alexmathers.net/5stbook
- Sign up to Alex's newsletter
- Click the download link in your email for instant download of the book

If you are looking for a simple list of five powerful reminders to help you uncover your unstoppable energy, this is the book for you.

INTRODUCTION

"Unfortunately, no one can be told what the Matrix is. You have to see it for yourself." — Morpheus

When I was young, I enjoyed performing magic shows for my family. I'd lock the door of my room, study, and practice my tricks, and then – donning my best attire – I would assume the role of the magician.

The thing I liked most wasn't being the centre of attention; it was seeing the joy in my family's faces, captivated as they were by the illusion that I was creating.

Today, as a writer and coach, I am driven to create magic, albeit in a slightly different way; but it is still magic, nonetheless. My work enables me to show others how magic is an integral part of our life experience, how much of a hold illusion has on us, and how we can liberate ourselves from the 'spells' that keep us bound.

Thank you for choosing this book and having faith in me as your guide. My goal is to help you see life through new eyes.

My hope is that this shift will help you renew or regain a more immediate sense of peace, joy, and optimism.

For some of you, the ideas I'm about to share will serve as helpful reminders. For others, they could change everything.

If you are currently experiencing any suffering, anxiety, or stress, rejoice, for this book may provide some relief.

Many of you may find these concepts challenging at first, especially if you have been following a different paradigm in life. But I ask that you consider this new paradigm with an open mind – a "Beginner's Mind," as they say in the Zen tradition – one that is open to what I'm about to share without preconceptions or judgement.

Criticism of the ideas contained here will only impede learning, possibly even rendering this reading a waste of time. But if you remain open and receptive, you will more easily grasp the truths conveyed in these words.

For whom is this book written?

This book does not target one particular reader. These concepts can equally benefit the artist, the CEO, the stay-at-home mother of four, and the farmer tending to his crop.

This is the kind of material that can be re-read, and dipped into as needed.

This is not a philosophy book.

In these pages, I will discuss very real natural laws that, when understood, will help you reach deeper mental wellness. This is a book about how we think; how our thinking directly shapes our experience of reality, and how this understanding impacts our mental health.

Before we delve into this, I must acknowledge the importance of a healthy diet, adequate sleep and exercise, since these factors contribute greatly to physical and mental health. However, they are often ignored in books that speak to the principles that I will share here.

Our thoughts create our emotional experiences. How we feel is determined by how we think. Nevertheless, physical health also influences how we feel via the filter of thought. Good health enables the entire system to work optimally.

Although the health of our minds is the overarching determinant of our experience and the focus of this book, it is based on a foundation of physical health upon which more profound benefits can be built.

I guarantee that if you are willing to absorb what I'm about to show you, let go of unhelpful assumptions, and allow your perspective to re-align with something new, you can live a peaceful and energised life, regardless of your circumstances.

With that in mind, make yourself comfortable, take a slow breath, and let's begin.

WHO IS ALEX MATHERS?

Who am I to make such bold claims?

Am I some mountain-dwelling monk who has found enlightenment?

Do I go through life in a state of continual and total bliss?

Do I think I have all the answers?

Am I in possession of a long, flowing white beard?

No, no, no, and... not yet.

I am human and fallible like everyone else but fortunate to have come across a set of principles that steer me back on track any time I wander.

Living by these principles means I am happier than I have ever been, and more often in a state of ease, creativity, and joy. I have a significantly more harmonious relationship with life and the way it unfolds.

I have not had a transformational enlightenment experience. I spent a large portion of my years in various degrees of depression, dissatisfaction, worry, and doubt.

In my late teens and twenties, I suffered from what I regarded as social anxiety, which stemmed from bullying at school. I was so nervous at work that my vision would become spotty and distorted during meetings.

As the perspectives discussed in this book became engrained deeper and deeper within me, over the last few years, I experienced a gradual shift that has led to more frequent and consistent wellness and peace.

The process does not have to take that long because, as we'll see here, there is only one requirement: understanding three fundamental building blocks, which reveal that you already have everything you need to be well.

"The principles are an attempt to explain the most fundamental, essential nature of the human experience." — George Pranksy

I have devoted a large portion of my life to understanding and resolving the suffering that I was experiencing, notably anxiety. I tried all kinds of techniques, hacks, and experiments such as meditation, special diets, cognitive behavioural therapy (CBT), homeopathic remedies, eye movement desensitisation and reprocessing (EMDR), emotional freedom tapping (EFT), and Neuro-inguistic programming (NLP).

Some things made a difference, but I rarely allowed real change to take root because I was always looking for something outside of me to "fix" what I thought was "wrong" with me.

By merely adopting the attitude of someone who needed fixing, I was inadvertently manufacturing the false idea that there was something wrong with me.

There was nothing wrong with me, just like there is nothing wrong with you.

Everything you need for total wellness is already within you.

I know this may sound cheesy to some, but please suspend your scepticism and continue reading.

It wasn't until I came across the three principles introduced by a Scottish welder named Syd Banks some years ago that things fell into place.

All that had shown signs of working for me in the past finally gained some definition. I had found a perspective that reduced what I had already vaguely known to be true to a purity that made complete sense to me.

Syd Banks is still relatively unknown, and this makes sharing his principles all the more exciting. His ideas form the foundation of the concepts in this book, although he is not the first or only person to have brought to the fore such universal truths about how humans experience reality.

Syd found a way to describe – in a profound, practical, and straightforward way – what many religious writings, spiritual teachers, and self-development guides have tried to impart, and which have been reflected in the findings of many physicists and scientists.

The three principles are not behavioural techniques or disciplines like EFT, NLP, CBT, energy healing, and hypnotherapy.

They do not constitute a philosophy that dictates how we should behave and what practices to undertake. They are not based on self-analysis, and there is no need to come to terms with your past.

They are not a motivational technique that paints over the deeper issues, nor is it about being more positive.

Syd's approach is concerned with understanding the fundamentals that make up the human experience and their implications on our wellbeing.

It is with the support of Syd's findings, as well as knowing myself and my own struggles, that I can help you.

We can do this together, over the course of this short book, by seeing how we limit ourselves by believing things that aren't real.

A NOTE ON SPIRITUALITY

This book does explore what many would call spirituality. I define spirituality as an acknowledgement of forces that operate outside our direct, measurable perception. That's it.

I am not a strict follower of any one religion but do refer to teachings from faiths that have come to similar or shared conclusions about many of the universal facts put forward in this book.

I ask those of you who do not consider yourselves spiritual or religious to stay open. It is not necessary to directly see, perceive, and confirm what I am proposing to realise that a basic understanding of these concepts could be the difference between mental torment and wellness.

That's worth your time, isn't it?

Before we go into the six beliefs, let's first look at the three principles more closely. Understanding these principles will set the stage to create more clarity for when I describe the six beliefs.

1

THE THREE PRINCIPLES

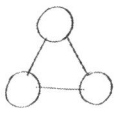

"Thought is not reality, yet it is through thought that our realities are created." — Sydney Banks

In the early 1970s, Syd Banks had a profound insight into the nature of thinking.

He realised that we live in a projected, subjective, continually changing, physical reality that emanates from our own minds.

Heavy stuff? Not necessarily. This may seem far out only because this is a new way of seeing for you — because you have never considered reality in those terms.

SYD TALKED about the three gifts that every human is endowed with that define the entirety of our experience. Understanding them allows us to achieve peace, inner wisdom, and creative power in our everyday lives.

His principles reveal that our thinking is the cause of all our problems.

Yes, all of them.

He called them principles because they are valid for everyone. They are not abstractions. They are universal truths, facts, constants, like gravity. And whether we believe them or not, they are always there.

The more you understand them and experience them objectively, the more they will register as true for you. We may not be able to measure the forces at play, but we can quantify the results that we see in ourselves when we operate in the full understanding of how they work.

Below are the principles in more detail. Don't feel you need to understand all of this right away. It can take time to assimilate these ideas.

You don't need to know the inner intricacies of this system to find wellness, either.

I'll be referring back to these as we go, so it's okay if you do not fully grasp these concepts right away. I didn't either.

First up, we have MIND.

The Mind is a higher order of intelligence. It's Mind with a capital "M" because it is universal rather than personal. It is the constant, connected, and intelligent energy force that brings about all existence. It is the force that turns acorns into oak trees, keeps the moon in place, and determines how bees create honeycombs.

> *"All matter originates and exists only by virtue of a force. We must assume behind this force the existence of a conscious and*

intelligent Mind. This Mind is the matrix of all matter." — Max Planck, Founder of Quantum Theory

Mind gives life to all things. It is the source of ongoing creative insight, well-being, and wisdom. It is continually available to us.

WE CAN USE the Mind in two ways:

FIRST, there is the constant, formless impersonal universal Mind. It can be understood as who we are in our default state; our innate being shared by all other beings. It is the pure creative energy of aliveness and it is impossible to truly describe in words because it is without form. We don't 'use' this Mind as such, rather, when we do not interfere, we can more clearly experience its continual flow of creation and intelligence. It is who we are in our purest sense, beyond identity.

It is us and all things.

SECOND, there is the personal mind. It is in a continual state of flux. The personal mind is significant because it describes the human tendency to take over manual control of the default universal Mind and apply additional thinking to provide solutions to the problems we seem to have. The personal mind in action is like a pilot manually commandeering a plane that has been flying on autopilot.

Though the personal mind – also called the "egoic mind" – can accomplish what we might describe as more practical things such as plan and design things, it also often uses thought in unhelpful ways. It can hold on to certain thoughts that create a (false) sense of who we are at a superficial level.

In this way, there are two selves in operation: the underlying, objective, connected, and universal Being, and the surface-level, subjective self with an ascribed identity.

The Universal Mind and the personal mind are not two minds that think differently. They are two ways of using the same mind.

As Syd says: *"Universal Mind is the mind you should be looking for. It's the Mind that has the power to guide you through life, and if you can see that, life becomes simple, and you'll find your happiness. Cause happiness is inside, honestly, it's inside."*

THE MIND IS NOT the same thing as the brain, as is often mistakenly assumed. The mind is purely energetic, whereas the brain is biological. The brain can be seen as a computer that accepts the input of programming. What you put into a computer, you get out of it. The Mind, however, is the intelligent life force and exists before form. We can compare it to a computer's operating system.

IF YOU HAVE trouble seeing how there could be such a thing as a universal intelligence, which we can't see or ever measure, ask yourself: "What is giving me the power to think at all?"

The second of the three principles is CONSCIOUSNESS.

A universal constant, Consciousness with a capital "C" is the gift of awareness. It allows us to experience everything from a bird flying by to a bug crawling on our hand to the sense of aliveness within us.

Our Consciousness gives us whatever experience our thoughts create, making that creation look and feel real. When you refer to physics, and study matter at the atomic level, we see that everything is literally composed of energy, in exactly the same way as thought is composed of energy. In this way, we are literally experiencing the energy of thought through our Consciousness.

> *"In this flow, mind and matter are not separate substances. Rather, they are different aspects of one whole and unbroken movement."* — David Bohm, Theoretical Physicist

Consciousness allows for the recognition of form. It is the space within which we experience all of existence. It is the arena of your own creation. It is the landscape providing us with the incredible opportunity to perceive our innate connectedness to all things through Mind; to see how we *are* all things. As physicist Paul Dirac said, *"pick a flower on Earth and you move the farthest star."*

BRAIN MELT WARNING: A lot of these ideas cannot simply be 'speed-read' once and understood. They require contemplation. These are not easy ideas for many, as they were not for me!

CONSCIOUSNESS, as Syd puts it, *"has infinite levels; you will never come to the end of Consciousness. It is impossible, because Consciousness is infinite. That's a beautiful thing to know because it means there is no end of you finding beauty, love, and understanding."*

Our levels of Consciousness change with our thinking as we see the world through different lenses of thought.

We can see things in one way and feel low as a result, or we can be in a great mood simply because we have allowed our thoughts to be still or because we have shifted our perspective to something refreshing and benign. Because everything is energy, reality literally refreshes - like when we reload a web-page - when your level of consciousness refreshes.

MENTAL HEALTH, joy, and happiness lie within everyone's consciousness but are obscured and held captive by our inaccurate, egoic thinking.

Now, we turn to the third principle of THOUGHT.

Our entire experience of form and sensation, moment by moment, is created by our thoughts.

Thought is the paintbrush that turns the invisible energy of universal Mind into forms, which are experienced as sensations like seeing and hearing, when painted onto the canvas of Consciousness.

The outside world cannot make us feel anything, unlike what the media or society repeatedly tell us. Nor can it affect our behaviour or performance. Only our thinking has the power to do this. Our thoughts create the entire reality that we experience. The outside world is, in this sense, our thinking.

How we see things affects the things that we see. For example, if we think of ourselves as shy around people, this

Illusory   7

is generating a reality in which people appear as a threat. This was how I lived for the longest time. In contrast, if we think of people as a source of intrigue, our experience of people will be exciting and interesting. We are only limited by our thinking.

> *"As water by cooling and condensation becomes ice, so thought by condensation assumes physical form. Everything in the universe is thought in material form."* — Paramahansa Yogananda

We can see thought as the most significant power at our disposal. It is the power to create anything. It gives us the ability to visualise, plan, and tell stories. It is a tool that we can use to create and innovate, or a means to judge and ruminate (via our personal mind).

Thought, on its own, is an entirely neutral gift.

Thoughts that arise from universal Mind enable our experience of Consciousness.

According to Syd, *"You're only one thought away from happiness; you're only one thought away from sadness. The secret lies in thought."*

YOU COULD SEE Mind as a projector, Consciousness as a screen on which reality is experienced, and Thought as the beam of light that completes the picture of what we experience. There is nothing you can perceive in the world that the three principles did not create.

The three principles interconnect at varying levels of purity. There is the total purity of universal Mind, universal Consciousness, and universal Thought. We all have the ability to tap into its purest, most fundamental state. We can see personal mind, personal consciousness, and personal thought reflecting rather more 'impure' versions of the same three components. They manifest as universal purity mixed in with our personal interpretations.

It is this "mix" that gives rise to suffering, as we will explore as we go further.

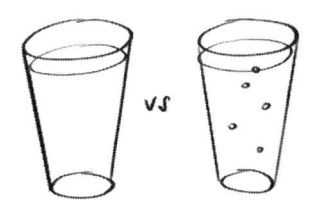

Universal 'purity' vs Personal 'impurity'

WHAT DOES all this have to do with mental well-being, joy, and happiness?

These principles reveal something that transformed every area of my life. I had gotten close in my years of experimentation and "fixing" but never realised how simple it was until I truly understood what implications these principles had.

Our thoughts create our experience in its entirety.

Our thinking directly affects how we feel, and our feelings impact our behaviours. Thinking, as Syd put it, is *"the missing link that gives us the power to recognise the illusory separation between the spiritual world and the world of form."*

Nothing in the world is the cause of what we think and how we feel.

It all comes from within. This is key.

No INCIDENT, person, or stimulation affects our experience directly. Everything runs through thought first. All experience, even physical pain is created through thought. How? Because our thoughts tell us if something is painful or not. There is a condition called Congenital Analgesia, in which people do not sense physical pain coming from outside stimuli because of a chemical imbalance in the brain. The imbalance leads to a shift in how sufferers interpret what for most should be painful. It leads to children receiving all kinds of injuries and broken bones more easily because they can't experience the pain that would otherwise keep them from being hurt. Because there are no thoughts telling them that there is a problem, they can't sense the pain.

Another example might be someone who hates being touched suffering through a massage and interpreting it as painful, whereas the person on the next table could be in ecstasy. It is the thought that precedes the feeling, always.

If someone pinches us, we feel the pinch as it is interpreted by our thoughts. The physical act of the pinch must first run through our lens of thought to create the feeling of pain. If someone says something seemingly offensive, it is not their words that we feel; we feel our interpretation of their words.

Understanding this dynamic is the key to the entire book, and the first step to mental wellness and unparalleled energy.

When we feel that something is "bad" out there, we are

feeling our own thought-created resistance to it, not the external thing itself.

We are in the experience of mind interacting with thought, interacting with consciousness. That's all there is.

WHAT WE SEE out there in the world is the manifestation of our shared Consciousness born out of a single, universal, connected Mind. It takes some contemplation to understand this fully. But when we truly grasp it, we realise how interconnected everything is, and then love and compassion for all things arise automatically from this realisation.

> *"The total number of minds in the universe is one. In fact, consciousness is a singularity phasing within all beings."* — Dr. Erwin Shrödinger, Nobel Prize-Winning Physicist

Our personal mind adds a layer of subjective interpretation (through thinking) onto this projection, which alters the experience further.

The universal Mind and personal mind intermingle to create our experience.

The less interference we create with our personal mind, the closer to pure Consciousness, well-being, and wisdom we will be.

Most of what we see and sense in the world – people, buildings, and nature – come out of the creative, intelligent Mind producing Thought that is manifested in Consciousness. A lot of our experiences, especially the negative ones, are born out of our erroneous ego-driven thinking interacting with Mind and Consciousness.

This has tremendous implications on how we experience the world, and how we can manage our emotional experience.

We have a choice in how much we allow our personal thinking to obscure the beauty of pure universal Consciousness, free of judgement and labels.

Please read that again.

We have a choice.

As we will see in the coming chapters, we really do create our realities with our thinking. Those who are "mentally free" are no longer in the controlling grasp of the kind of egoic thinking that creates stress – the stress that obscures the joy, wisdom, and ease that lie beneath.

We will see how, for too long, we have attempted to change our *behaviours* as a way to counteract our increasing rate of mental suffering.

These principles possess such power because they look at what *makes* us human rather than what humans *do*; they examine the *root* not the *surface*.

We will explore six beliefs that demonstrate how our personal thinking can be innocently misused, thereby blocking us from having a beautiful and enlivening experience in all areas of life.

The six beliefs are:

1. I experience burnout because I work too much (work).
2. I'm a coward because I am feeling fear (fear).
3. The loss of net worth means a loss of self-worth (money).

4. When others reject me, my self-esteem decreases (people).
5. I must be in a good mood to perform well (performance).
6. My past defines my personality (personality).

Yes, these may seem arbitrary and narrow. But they are useful doorways into understanding the broader human experience and the mental health that is uncovered when we can transcend this thinking.

Let's dive into the first one...

2

BELIEF 1: I EXPERIENCE BURNOUT BECAUSE I WORK TOO MUCH

"If you really want to escape the things that harass you, what you're needing is not to be in a different place but to be a different person." — Seneca

I remember feeling extremely stressed a few years ago while preparing for a talk that I had to give to four hundred people in Barcelona. Days before the speech, I had all kinds of ideas floating around in my mind, but no structure or plan for my talk. My printer was acting up. I hadn't yet booked my flight. I was anxious about speaking in front of so many people with so little experience. I wasn't sure whether the organisers would appreciate what I had to share, worrying that they'd be resentful if I showed up in such a state. I was experiencing burnout before I'd even gone to the event!

The very real stress that I was feeling was a response to the thoughts in my head. None of the above was causing my stress directly. Some of it hadn't even happened yet. My personal mind was clouding my vision with distressing thoughts.

Worry was a misguided means of exerting some control over the situation. But this didn't help; it only strengthened the intensity of the negative thoughts, which created more stress, tightness, and anxiety.

REMEMBER, our thoughts create our feelings. Thoughts come first, and what we feel and experience comes second. When we feel burnout, stress, or whatever we think the appropriate label may be at the moment, we can easily be seduced into believing that something circumstantial and external to us is the cause.

But it's you.

We can't catch stress from our surroundings like the flu. We always create the stress in our minds via thought. It's all self-generated.

When we understand how we are creating our own experience through the three principles, we have the power to return to well-being, regardless of the circumstances.

We do this by grasping the internal workings of the human operating system. We realise how we are creating our stress by continually latching on to painful thoughts, ruminating, and clouding the innate wisdom and wellness that lie beneath.

This means that we need not cling to thoughts that don't serve us. We allow our breathing to slow down. We relax our shoulders and open ourselves to the task or person in front of us.

When viewed this way, stress becomes optional; it is no longer "a necessary burden" in our work. We realise that what we call stress is just one label for an energy, which could be given any other name. Perhaps it's excitement or a playful energy. Perhaps it's anticipation.

It's all energy either way. But because we are identifying with our thoughts and the labels they create, by considering it stress, we create a physical response to that interpretation.

But what if a deadline really is approaching?

What if people are counting on me to deliver? The fact that I had to give an important speech hadn't changed.

Didn't I need to feel pressure to complete what needed to be done?

No, I did not need to feel pressure, I needed to be present. I needed to engage with what I had in my power to attend to, rather than incapacitating myself with worrying thoughts. I needed to understand the nature of fluctuating mental energy – that thoughts come and go whether I like it or not. They can be helpful or unhelpful. What felt like anxiety may have come and gone in response to those thoughts, but that was all that was happening. Trouble will arise when we take unhelpful thoughts seriously. I needed to let go and return to the work in front of me, taking one step at a time.

Had I returned to the present without judging the work or myself, I would have been more at ease. I would have had a quieter mind, which would have delivered more creative insight from the well of universal Mind. Perhaps, I would have received the insight from universal Mind that this was an exciting and fun challenge, rather than a source of stress. I sure could have used that insight back then!

Pressure is only pressure when we label it as such. We can choose to see that same energy as life force rushing through us, as something that can contribute to the completion of our task. When we shift our thinking to something more benign – something that feels better emotionally – we raise our consciousness.

There is a source of constant innate intelligence in being conscious. By not becoming trapped in unhelpful thoughts, I could have created the space needed to receive the insights and clarity that would help me plan a powerful talk.

Being present isn't about *trying* to be present because that is self-conscious. It's about letting go of the part of us that doesn't want to be conscious. It's about getting into the feeling of what we're doing. It's about allowing our impersonal Mind to guide us.

When we are right there, away from the past or the future, tending to the thing in front of us, we are at our most resourceful, energised, and creative. It is not worth thinking about the items on our to-do list because there is nothing we can do to address them in the moment. There is relief in seeing that.

All we have is the present moment and what we can do right now. All else is unnecessary suffering.

Presence – away from the stories running in my mind – is what was required of me more than anything. Being present is to be conscious. It is to bask in the purity of conscious form all around us that has sprung from universal Mind.

But what if *unhelpful thoughts return?*

Thoughts will come and go continually. For thoughts to arise in the periphery of our minds is to be human. When we understand this, we can let them continue doing what they do without our clinging or interfering. There is freedom there, regardless of thoughts arising.

If you have known only your subjective thinking all your life, this takes some getting used to, but freedom is available to us in an instant. You will be your most creative when you are mentally still, conscious, and in flow – in physical motion with your work.

The more we can connect with the universal Mind beneath this cloud of self-protective thinking, the less constricted we are.

Become life force

Now, what I see allows me to live in the expression of my limitlessness more often, meaning that I tap into my inner force. So, rather than sitting idly like a monk in a monastery because I have "found myself," I make full use of the relentless energy swirling within me to create, build, share, and love in greater volume, and with greater intensity.

I know that I am okay and perfect just the way I am. So, when I create anything, I am doing it from a place of wholeness, rather than a sense of lack that requires me to do and have more so that I become a "better" person.

Operating in a fluid motion and allowing our thinking to settle are part of the same loop. As such, we need not start with a still mind. We can set the loop into motion by stepping into action right away. We can lean into a situation without thinking about it too much.

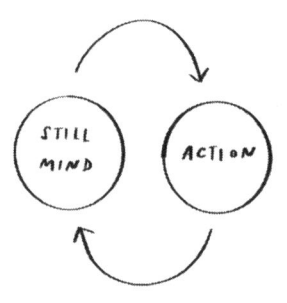

Through action, we are getting out of our heads, out of planning. When we are in movement and flow, we are the expression of our Universal Being. Give yourself a moment to sense the undercurrent of energy running through you, and you will know what this means.

Can't we make ourselves physically ill by working too hard?
We ought to acknowledge that stress can affect our health detrimentally. It isn't working hard per se that makes us ill, in this instance. We are thinking ourselves ill. It is all mental. What we think determines our feelings of anxiety and stress, and when we do it enough, it can lead to real physical and chemical changes. Take, for example, studies done on the detrimental health effects of loneliness. It is not the isolation that is creating health problems in the person in question. How can it be? It's all interpretation. It is what thoughts they are allowing themselves to take seriously. The thinking about there being a 'problem', or lack thereof, is what determines how someone who is isolated reacts emotionally and physically. Some people have lived healthy and happy lives for decades alone in the woods. Others can't bear being alone for a few hours.

We need to listen to our bodies to know when we need to rest. If how we think creates stressful feelings in us, we need to be aware of how we feel, since this could manifest into more severe physical issues.

Once we understand that it is our interpretation of what is happening that creates the stress that leads to illness, instead of the work itself, we are free. We are open to doing whatever we feel called to do with extra gusto. The more conscious we are in our pursuits, the less we will expend our energies unnecessarily on non-fruitful tasks.

"Stop acting so small. You are the universe in ecstatic motion."
— Rumi

There are countless stories of people who have performed tremendous physical and emotional feats that show how far we can extend our potential. These achievements also demonstrate how much we can limit ourselves by building walls of thought around us.

Apparent geniuses, prolific artists, or high-achieving athletes consistently thrive because they have found a way to tap into universal Mind. They have acquired the skill of tuning out much of their surface-level thinking so that an astonishing degree of knowingness can rise up through the spaces.

BUT ISN'T BEING CONTINUALLY *busy a waste of time, a waste of life?*

It depends on why and how you do what you do. It can be easy to fall into being busy for the sake of being busy, which isn't very efficient. I am always aware of the need to leverage my efforts for greater rewards. I am continually following my inner guidance system to create more productively. For example, when writing emails, I know that my time is better spent in the engaged writing of emails with my supporters or potential clients, over rushing through responding to all emails without discernment over which recipient requires closer care and attention, and which others require no response at all. It's not about working smarter; it's about working more consciously.

Getting back what I put in at a 1:1 ratio is not efficient in the long run and will lead to a continually low reward "busywork" for the effort invested. The ideal trajectory is to combine efficiency in our reward-to-effort ratio while being (genuinely living) in our energy force. It is to be both efficiently productive and energised.

The more I move and create, the more momentum and creative energy come through. Getting into motion and action (out of the mind and into the body) helps us bypass floundering thinking. From here, we will surprise ourselves with what is possible.

This isn't to say that slowing down and resting occasionally are bad things. There is a time for reflection and stillness. Creative motion and rest go hand-in-hand. To oscillate between flow and rest is to live.

All of us can enjoy an expression of playful, flowing, and open engagement. It is about throwing ourselves into it all, and seeing the enjoyment in it, no matter how mundane the task may be. Not because we're trying to get somewhere, or we have something to prove but because being a force of nature is the purest expression of our connection to universal Consciousness. Oh, and it makes things a lot more fun, too.

This is possible for everyone in all things. We can create with joy, and without burnout by understanding how the mind works, by letting go of unhelpful thoughts, and by allowing our innate wisdom to guide us more often.

We are free when we realise that we are physically and mentally only as limited as we think we are.

Things outside of us have no meaning. We apply meaning to them because we have the power of thought. As such, we can see reality any way we choose to see it, so we might as well see our world as a massive, enlivening opportunity for fun, challenge, service, adventure, and joy.

You don't have burnout because you work too much. You experience burnout because you react to all that thinking!

BELIEF 2: I'M A COWARD BECAUSE I FEEL FEAR

"When I let go of what I am, I become what I might be." — Lao Tzu

I've had a lot of trouble over the years feeling at ease when speaking in groups. At school, I was painfully afraid to contribute in class. As I grew older, that fear developed into anxiety, creating all kinds of unnecessary and restrictive suffering that held me back from sharing my real and alive self. For years, I couldn't forgive myself because I believed that I was cowardly for not contributing in groups at school.

If you asked me back then why this was happening, I would have told you the story that I had made up for myself – that I was shy, different from other people, not a natural or expressive speaker, an introvert, an anxious person in groups. I would have told you that I had "social anxiety."

All lies. All subjective interpretations. All judgements. All thoughts. All attempts at creating meaning where there was none.

I took my thoughts seriously. I believed what they were

telling me about myself, defining who I was – nothing more, nothing less.

Those thoughts created a feeling of nervousness in me. But it went a step further. Feeling slightly nervous is one thing, but I would often experience full-blown anxiety in anticipation of and during an event. In my seemingly noble desire to be without fear, I resisted any sense of fear that came up. And so, the cycle continued.

We can interpret our feelings to mean that "something is wrong with us," thereby applying more pressure, via our thinking, to end those feelings. Our egos want nothing to do with those uncomfortable, embarrassing feelings. So we resist. And this creates more pressure and intensifies our anxiety.

What can we do to release this pressure?

We can understand and accept the self-created, fluctuating nature of mental energy.

We can accept that thoughts, which are out of our control, will come up and that they are transient and meaningless. We can realise that we need not follow what they are telling us and that we can create space in our thinking by returning to presence. We need not resist the physical feelings that negative thoughts evoke in us.

Simply put: When we feel a negative emotion arise in us, be it frustration, sadness, or anxiety, we don't have to resist it. To resist feeling is to add to more thinking, and this will only add more pressure.

MANY TIMES, the feelings that arise in us can help keep us alert, especially when interpreted as helpful, and merely as energy. We can be with the feelings, to welcome them. They may hurt initially, but they will dissolve on their own, much like a thought dissolves when we don't hold on tight.

We can acknowledge the transience and impermanence of thought and be present with them as they come and go.

To think or focus our way out of feeling bad is futile; it will only stir our thinking further, creating an emotionally-adverse reaction.

We need to be open to whatever the present moment offers. We need to be conscious with it and breathe through it. To lean into moments like these can take courage. It is easy to fall into the trap of reacting to our emotions, to snap at someone when we feel anger; to enter into a cycle of anxiety.

But this is our opportunity for growth, to be at ease with the situation, to let go of feelings that come up, and to see that we are not our feelings. Feelings reflect our transient, often nonsensical thinking. That's it.

Feelings are superb indicators of our state of mind. If we feel good, we know that our thinking is where it needs to be. If we feel bad, we know we are unconscious. We are in our thoughts. We can use our feelings as signposts that direct us to the need to be more present.

If we feel bad, we're overthinking. We're allowing our personal mind to interfere and ruminate. It's time to return to stillness, to let innate wisdom arise and guide us back to wellness, as it does so well.

If I find myself in a group setting today, something that feels like anxiety may return, but now I welcome it. I smile at the flawed stories that arise out of the personal, egoic mind and its need for self-preservation. I allow it to come and go like a quirky house mate in my mind who is doing his thing. It is nothing to resist or take personally.

I know that if I had negative thoughts and felt bad in the past, that didn't make me wrong. If I have a negative mood today, that does not make me a person that needs fixing. It just makes me human.

Many of us feel shame for how we thought, felt, and behaved in the past. We think that our fearful thoughts, which led to fearful behaviour, have defined who we are. We think that we were cowards, losers, or failures, but that is a profoundly inaccurate self-assessment. Our behaviour had nothing to do with who we were. It had to do with how we were thinking. Maybe we didn't understand the nature of thought at the time. We were unaware that all we had to do was not take our thinking so seriously.

Forgive yourself

Give yourself a moment to find compassion for yourself again. Forgive yourself. Know that you were acting in a way that made total sense to you, given the thinking that was creating your reality at the time. You did your best, given what was on your mind. The same goes for people you may be having trouble forgiving. They were doing the best, given their thinking at the time. It's never personal.

We create suffering by believing the illusion of thoughts to be an objective reality when it is, in fact, created by our subjective minds.

Looking at the content of our thoughts is not necessary. All we need to see is that we have the power to think, and that thought has the potential to create our emotional experience.

I find a way to love what is here with me. I use this moment as an opportunity to let go, to feel the life force running through me, to breathe, and to direct my attention away from myself (self-conscious) and towards those others in the room with me (conscious).

Rather than believing that our negative thoughts and feelings are an indication of what's "wrong" with us, we can see that they are simply real-time, physical reflections of our transient thinking.

Truly seeing this changes everything.

BELIEF 3: LOSS OF NET WORTH MEANS A LOSS OF SELF-WORTH

"If you're doing things in order to be happy, you're doing them in the wrong order." — Michael Neill.

If you asked every adult on earth to list their biggest challenges, I bet that one of the most common complaints – if not the most common – would be money.

We worry that we don't have enough to pay our bills. And we are anxious about losing the money we do have. Even when we have more than enough, we fear losing it and pine after more.

"I'll be happy when I have an extra couple of grand coming in each month," we say. And we never quite get to the amount that feels satisfying.

We live on a planet that runs on money. We rely on money to survive, exchange, and get what we need to support ourselves and our families. Surely this means we need to take it seriously. Survival is at stake. Health is at stake!

Right?

Many do take money seriously. Many even view it as having a damaging and corrupting influence.

It doesn't. Money holds no meaning whatsoever. Money is neither good nor bad, just like all the circumstantial phenomena that I've spoken about so far – be it public speaking, deadlines, endless to-do lists, and so on. These are neutral phenomena unfolding within the theatre of shared universal Consciousness.

So is money.

Money is a tool. It has no meaning other than the meaning we attach to it.

As we've seen so far, we tend to apply certain beliefs to the world around us in ways that don't serve us. These beliefs could have been formed in all kinds of ways, from things our parents said, to cultural programming to the films we watch.

None of it matters. At their purest essence, beliefs are thoughts that arise moment by moment that we needn't even acknowledge.

Several beliefs prevent people from making money more freely and from being at peace with the idea of wealth. A common belief is that making money will make us happy. In other words, if we lose money, we lose happiness, self-worth, or joy. All this effectively means the same thing: We take money personally. We tie money to ourselves.

This is what our egos do. We create an identity through things that exist outside ourselves because we fail to understand our inner Being, our universal identity – that which is connected to all things.

Many people have become rich with the belief that their happiness will increase as they make more money. What a superb incentive that is! But it's also a great reason to jump off a bridge should that money be lost suddenly. And this has happened many times.

Interestingly, and what might be less obvious despite that it affects many people, is the aversion to making money because we believe we'll see our happiness decrease if we were to be denied new money or lose it.

This is a common reason why so many stay poor. It may not be because of their circumstances or because they don't know how to make money. Many people do know how. We have Google. We have countless books and resources and gurus.

People fail to go out into the marketplace to make money because they tie money to self-worth, to their identity. We have fear or we avoid making it because that puts us at risk of losing ourselves. We risk damage to our illusory self-worth.

Whatever the underlying reason, none of it matters anyway, because the resistance we have to money comes in the form of a thought. A thought is a tool. In and of itself, it is meaningless, subjective; it is energy.

Knowing this, we can let go of the thought and return to being present, free of thought interference, back to the realisation that we are already whole. Perhaps, in one such moment of clarity, the insight emerges that we can see money as an indication of the difference we are making in the world. It is a means that can bring about positive change.

That makes sense, seeing that money is essentially a token of thanks given in exchange for value received. Money can be used directly for good.

We can see money as the "root of all evil," or as an "indication of making a difference in the world."

Which would you choose? Which understanding would be more conducive to making more money and enjoying the process?

UNDERSTANDING the three principles and the nature of thought shows us that stress around money comes from our thinking, not from the loss of money itself. We can then give ourselves some space by stilling the mind and being rewarded by the innate intelligence, which provides us with the resourcefulness to make more when we need it.

In the past, I would wake up during the night in a cold sweat about money. I would worry and ruminate for hours before falling asleep. The problem seemed very real and immediate.

As I have allowed more stillness to replace unhelpful visions in my mind over the years, these moments have become rare and short-lived. If I am facing a particularly thorny money-related challenge, I set it aside. My inner wisdom eventually provides the answer I need.

When we realise that money is in no way connected to our sense of worth or happiness, we can be freer with it. It becomes like Monopoly money. It becomes a game where we are less attached to winning. We are no longer in awe of it.

If we want to earn more money, it will greatly serve us to see money in this way. We can't fear losing it. We need to take risks. We need to be willing to ask people for it and be denied it as part of that journey.

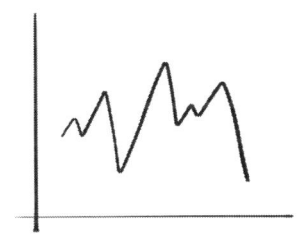

We need to be okay with seeing our shares drop, knowing that we will be happy right now regardless. This is not to say that we should be reckless, lose control, and all our money along with it. We will make more creative and appropriate money decisions because we're not clouding our soul's intelligence with worry.

Like in other chapters, the implications are similar. If we can see that we are not our thoughts concerning something external, we do not have to be limited by that thing. We can be free to live as an expression of who we are without a sense of being limited by money. We can create as much money and wealth as we want.

Without the limitation of thought, and in choosing to live in playful motion rooted to inner wisdom, we might be surprised at how much money we can make as a reflection of the positive difference we're making in the world.

What a way to look at money!

And that's what this is all about: We can view things in any way we choose. Money doesn't have to be a burden, something that creates stress and fear. We don't need to put on the brakes, if we feel we're making too much of that "evil paper."

It can be viewed as a neutral tool but also as a benevolent one – one that can create positive and charitable change in the world. In that sense, the more we make, the more good we can do.

All the happiness we would ever need is already within us. All that is left is to see money-creation for the game that it is.

Have fun.

BELIEF 4: IF OTHERS REJECT ME, MY SELF-ESTEEM DECREASES

"Only you can take inner freedom away from yourself, or give it to yourself. Nobody else can." — Michael A. Singer

All my life, I worried about what other people would think of me.

The fear of being judged can be all-consuming and a significant source of needless suffering.

Earlier in this book, I said that I developed social anxiety as a result of being bullied at school and of the heavy self-criticism that accompanied it. Knowing what you now know, you can see that only my mental interpretation of events could have led to my insecurities later in life. This means that the bullying, in and of itself, had no impact on what I perceived to be anxiety later on in life. There is tremendous freedom and relief in understanding this. Funnily enough, some of those I considered bullies back then are among close friends today.

I felt anxiety any time I resisted the thoughts and feelings that arose out of my mental state and associated memories. Anxiety can only exist when we identify with our thoughts, when we are not present, when we are unconscious. In this way, anxiety isn't even a "thing," unless we make it so.

We can, therefore, become ourselves again when we turn to Consciousness. It is in the presence of Consciousness that the pure creative energy of universal Mind can heal and guide us.

Thoughts can be addictive, and this is why this takes some cultivating. It means continually returning to the stillness of mind by being more aware that there is more (way, way more!) to us beyond our egoic-mind.

A note on physical health:

As I mentioned earlier, eating, sleeping well, and keeping our physical bodies in good order are essential for wellness. These factors play a role in our experience of mental health.

However, this doesn't change the universal fact that we create our entire experience through the lens of thought. Thought creates the sensation of anxiety, especially if we label it as such. If our bodies are healthy, but we have tormenting thoughts, we can experience anxiety. If our bodies are unhealthy, however, any tension that we feel via fearful thoughts can be amplified even more.

Therefore, maintaining robust physical health is key. The beauty of this is that, when you listen to your innate intelligence, it will guide you to what your body needs.

Don't we become less confident when others criticise or reject us?

We can very easily be tempted to think that we lose a piece of ourselves when others say harsh things to us. The pain of an insult feels very real. Our self-esteem goes down. We lose confidence.

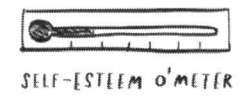

SELF-ESTEEM O'METER

This is all untrue. Other people cannot possibly have any direct effect on who we are.

We are already confident beneath the illusion of outer identity.

Our momentary feelings merely reflect the fleeting thoughts that we have instant to instant. Understanding this can be liberating for the majority of people who take rejection and the sense of abandonment very seriously.

If we absorb the idea that what others say has no impact whatsoever on our self-esteem (which is a thought-created illusion), what does that do to our ability to express ourselves and be our most creative and playful selves when we might otherwise experience fear of judgement?

We really can become untouchable in this sense. We need not be limited by what others do or say or believe.

Simply by understanding how this works, my life has changed dramatically. I can experience nerves in some settings, of course, but I can also view those nerves as an expression of excitement. I can end the spiral of anxiety triggered by specific environments by accepting my transient feelings, and allowing myself to *be* rather than by trying to be "more relaxed" or anyone other than myself.

WE ARE ONLY as worthy as we think we are. This changes moment to moment as a result of – not the environments and the people we find ourselves with – but the fluctuations in our thoughts that lead to our emotional experience in those moments.

When we realise that we can let go of our thoughts, we free ourselves from the false perception that other people have any power over how we feel.

The personal or egoic-mind creates suffering because it generates the illusion that we are separate, isolated entities floating around in a cosmic spew. The personal mind is all about self-preservation, looking good, and not making mistakes because it views itself as separate. It ultimately fears death because it believes itself (the identity) to be a thing when it is merely an illusion.

The universal Mind, on the other hand, is connected to all other conscious beings. It ties together all existence at the level of Being, or what Eckart Tolle calls the "Oneness" of all things. There is an indescribable sense of harmony and connection that arises within us when we align with this unchanging and undying Mind.

Whether you believe in it or not, what matters is that this mind-created illusion of separateness only hurts us. When we live as expressions of this connectedness, everything changes. Life becomes an exciting opportunity to live our connectedness by *giving* rather than taking. It becomes an existence rooted in joyous unity with our fellow human, such that what we share, we receive.

Illusory

When you feel low, you are likely taking something personally, falling for the perverse wishes of your ego. You are in self-preservation mode, as a result of falling for the delusion of your fragile separateness.

When I feel depressed or anxious, I know that there is something I am taking too seriously. I am making this about me. I have fallen for some lie put forward by my ego. I am a victim of circumstance.

When we are triggered, that is the time to breathe, thank our feelings for showing us the way, and adopt a refreshed manner of giving

---

FOCUSING ON HELPING OTHERS, truly serving, and being a force for good in the world, is the antidote to much anxiety, depression, and sadness.

If I feel like I'm not receiving enough from others, whether in the form of love or business or respect, I look to where there may be a deficiency in my willingness to give, love or listen without expecting anything in return.

When we do this, we get out of our heads; our attention is directed outwards, towards others. We are leaders, guides, and nurturers of people and communities.

What if I just can't find real compassion for others? People seem so heartless and destructive. Why should I love them?

We *can* find ways to be compassionate. Other people are doing the best they can, given the way they see their realities in the moment. They may also be taking themselves too seriously. They may also be suffering. In fact, we are all usually experiencing varying degrees of confusion, concern, distress and fear. We're all as in awe of our experience of life as the next person. The way to live is from compassion for others and ourselves – to live in the full expression of our connected Universal Being.

This is the way to heal the insecurity we find when we're self-conscious, depressed, or lost.

Look to lift others.

BELIEF 5: I NEED THE RIGHT MINDSET TO PERFORM WELL

"Don't think. Thinking is the enemy of creativity. It's self-conscious, and anything self-conscious is lousy." — Ray Bradbury

For most of my life, I believed that I needed to have the right mindset to do well, that I needed to know how to think to be better, perform better, create better.

Guess what?

It doesn't help. It's not true. It's just an opinion, a thought that doesn't necessarily serve.

What does "mindset" mean, anyway?

IN UNDERSTANDING THE THREE PRINCIPLES, we come to see that our thinking determines our emotional experience. If a negative thought floats up, we will momentarily feel the experience of that thought. But then a new thought will come up to replace it. If an enlightened thought floats up, we will feel its calming spirit.

These thoughts are transient, ever-changing, and beyond our control. As our thoughts are ever shifting, so is our experience of reality. In this way, our emotional experience is also beyond our control.

We can, however, experience more well-being more of the time when we allow our thinking to improve by itself. Thoughts will always be there, but the less we try and interfere, the less we try to figure out how best to think, the more spacious and benign they become.

Where's the proof of this working?

Leave your thoughts alone (when you don't need them for creating and planning), and you will know and feel it.

Even when we are trying to think positively, we are thinking. This may bring about momentary good feelings, but there is still ultimately the sense that there is something that we need to change. It isn't about forcing change. It's about allowing what we need to come through effortlessly when we cease to "try" to do anything. When we try to think differently to feel better, the opposite happens. We become more self-conscious, and this will limit performance.

Our thoughts will come and go. Interfering in any way stirs our thinking and disrupts the flow of our natural authenticity.

When I was in my early teens, I lived in Barbados with my family. My dad was a British diplomat stationed there. It was on this tropical island that I first played golf, sometimes joining my father for a game on weekend mornings.

I found golf to be one of the most infuriating sports but also supremely satisfying when I hit the ball well. The trouble was, I couldn't put my finger on what made that difference. Sometimes I'd be in a good mood, feeling calm and satisfied from a prior successful hole. I'd stride to the tee and confidently swing the ball into the trees. Other times, I'd be fuming and annoyed, thinking about how difficult the game was, and strike the perfect chip onto the green.

What I have learned from playing golf and engaging in any task is that we can perform well even if we're not in the mood. Mood, in and of itself, has little bearing on performance. If we strike the ball well, we hit it well, regardless of how we feel at that moment. I've written some of my strongest articles when a little angry.

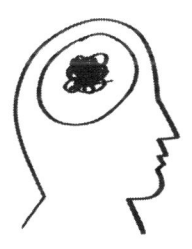

What does matter, however, is whether we're letting our thoughts settle or we are stirring them up by trying to act a certain way, by trying to improve our mindset. When I wasn't trying to think in any particular way but simply played or wrote or spoke, I tended to do better.

THE MISTAKE many sports coaches make is thinking that if we're not playing well, it's time for a mindset shift. It's time for a new game plan, like visualising success, being more focused, psyching ourselves up to be more aggressive, or calming ourselves down. This involves interference of some sort and will likely lead to self-consciousness.

Self-consciousness runs counter to what we need, which is stillness of mind.

Therefore, the secret to high performance in all things is to *feel* our way into what it is we're doing. We can use the action itself to get out of our minds and into the movement and sensation of our bodies and our surroundings.

We can be in a terrible mood when we start an activity but feel our way into performing well. But we cannot think or focus our way into feeling good so that we will perform better.

Consider this next time you need to perform, whether it's speaking in public, playing tennis, or writing a blog post. If you aren't feeling "optimally," don't try to do anything in particular to get to where you think you should be.

All this does is apply unnecessary pressure. This is the time to let your mind do the work while you get into motion. It may help you to follow your breath for a while or notice the sensations in your body.

> *"It's the place where there is freedom; where athletes don't think, they know; they don't focus, they feel. They don't grind, they allow."* Damian Mark Smyth

When I start writing, for example, I don't always feel in the mood, but that is not a reason not to write. I simply see how I feel as an indication of how I'm thinking and go from there. That's the time to loosen up through writing – writing anything, even if it's total crap – just to get into the flow. I let go of trying to think in an intelligent way; instead, I allow my inner wisdom to deliver the answers as I go, even if this means having to delete a lot of extraneous material later. Rather than feeling we need to be in the best mood to start something, we can view the very task or performance at hand to mould us into who we need to be to do it well.

If I need to perform publicly, I don't try to psych myself up. I don't visualise who I need to be, nor do I repeat affirmations to get my mind into a particular space. I just let go, take it all in, and feel my way into the moment.

This is not to say that visualisation is not a powerful tool in our mental toolbox for creating things. It is. But in the sphere of physical performance, it serves us more to revert to stillness of mind and the wisdom that will come through automatically. I may do some power poses, because that is physical, in the body, rather than thought-driven. I take the strain off my thinking by immersing myself in the sensations around me or by deeply listening to others.

Genius appears when we're in motion, not when we're clinging to our thoughts.

BELIEF 6: MY PAST DEFINES MY PERSONALITY

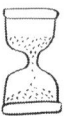

"The past gives you an identity and the future holds the promise of salvation, of fulfilment in whatever form. Both are illusions." — Eckart Tolle

Isn't it extraordinary how much of a hold the past can have on us?

My clients tell me things like: "I was humiliated by my teacher in class, so now I am fearful of being assertive," or "Because my mother never said she loved me, I am unable to love myself," or "My family never went travelling when we were young, so now I am fearful of overseas travel."

We can have the belief that past events, and how we felt and behaved at specific points in our history, somehow define who we are today. The past appears to us as a fixed, objective truth that has the power to determine who we are.

Some experiences have been run through our heads so many times that they can feel like trauma. It's like they've left a physical weight or internal blisters.

The feelings that we have today are only responses to

thoughts in the moment. We are not responding to reality when we feel triggered, because there is no objective reality, only an experience of a reality. What we are feeling are habitual thoughts that create our experience. And those thoughts do not need to define us.

I certainly believed in this delusion for a long time. We can be prisoners of our past. We can be sitting in a cell without realising that the door is unlocked, waiting to be pushed open.

For most of my life, the past dominated my actions in the present. I believed that the things that I and others did influenced who I became.

Because I was reserved in classes at school, I couldn't shake off being defined by this artificial, shy "personality." I believed that I was doomed to conform to a morose and expressionless personality for the rest of my life or until I "fixed" myself. This was a very real image that I held in my head, a shame that I carried around with me. I felt a potent influence over my behaviour when I held on to these thoughts in many settings. I seized up and kept quiet around people. I found myself being serious and glum around others when I didn't need to be.

All this because of a story that I held about the kind of person I was. You guessed it: It was a lie, and I fell for it.

WHEN WE HOLD a certain belief about who we are, we go about making sure that this belief is proven with our actions and reflected in the world around us. We behave, act, and experience the reality of our beliefs. I'm sure you can see how backward this is.

This also applies to any thought-driven belief that we

currently hold about what we are capable of and who we are.

I was speaking to a client recently about making money from her designs. In talking with her, it emerged that she held the belief that no one would be willing to pay good money for the illustrations she created. She had been looking for confirmation of this false truth in her world, finding it, and consequently not being paid well.

I helped her see that – by realizing the falseness of this belief and understanding how the opposite might be true – she could find people to pay well for her work. With this refreshed perspective, she was able to approach willing buyers with much less resistance.

Now that I understand the three principles and the futility of unhelpful thinking, I see the ludicrousness of the idea that my past defines me. Seeing the absurdity of the beliefs that we hold to be true enables us to let them go.

By seeing the illusion of my 'self' as the lie that it was, I am free to be myself. This has helped me question all my beliefs, break them down, and look at them from different perspectives. We can see all beliefs from different angles – that's how they work. Or we can let them go altogether. Beliefs are never objective truths.

When we understand this, we become free to view ourselves in any way we want. By recognising the subjectivity in all this, I elevate my consciousness.

"A thought is harmless unless we believe it. It's not our thoughts, but our attachment to our thoughts, that causes suffering. Attaching to a thought means believing that it's true, without

inquiring. A belief is a thought that we've been attaching to, often for years." — Byron Katie

When we live in the warm light of universal Mind, which lies beneath the mesh of stories and judgements created by the personal mind, we receive the gift of authenticity, real energy, and natural expression without fear of judgement.

It is in the seemingly paradoxical state of not knowing who we are that we can embark on the adventure of truly being ourselves.

Many of us feel that we need to "figure ourselves out" to find wellness, dig into our turbulent pasts to learn more about the trauma so we can finally "fix" ourselves.

None of this is required.

Every time we feel that our past has a hold on us is, we slip into the habit of taking our thoughts seriously. Seeing that this is possible is hugely liberating. When we buy into a particular story about who we are and how our past has defined us, we live in the experience of that reality, as conceived by the three principles of Mind, Consciousness, and Thought.

The opposite is possible, of course, when we have the strength and understanding to allow fluctuating mental energy to move through us with minimal influence.

THERE WILL BE situations when specific thoughts or feelings will be triggered quite powerfully. Eckhart Tolle calls this the activation of the "pain-body." The pain-body is experienced when we run across a thickly-accumulated collection of associated thoughts, like closely-entwined fibres that can quickly catch fire.

This is why certain thoughts feel so real, so physical. But the dynamic at play is the same. We are feeling the experience created by thinking moment to moment. The solution is to let go of those thoughts. This is challenging when the pain-body is more substantial, but we must find the courage to lean into things that feel uncomfortable. We must practice opening ourselves to the present and being there, rather than allowing ourselves to replay those thoughts and resist what's happening. This is how we expand our souls and explore our potential.

This isn't about being someone you're not, nor is it about trying to smile or relax. When you try to do anything, you are applying pressure. To move past what tends to scare or trigger you, you need only *not* resist.

With the creativity, joy, and presence that come from this unfiltered, default state, you will see your true self emerging.

The less we resist, the more we breathe through the resistance, and the more present we become. The less energy we give to these thoughts, the more we open a gap for peace to return. This is how we can dissolve the pain-body over time.

In this way, we can see our entire lives as an opportunity to expand, grow, and give.

Over the coming moments, you may find it useful to notice when you resist, when you scrunch your brow in response to something that feels real. Notice when you get angry. Practice non-resistance at those moments; let it go. You will grow in these moments. There is tremendous power and transformation when you adopt this as an ongoing practice.

The power of forgiveness

You are bringing forth the same loving energy when you are grateful for what you have, or when you forgive others and yourself. Forgiveness is essentially letting go of harmful thinking, and doing so is healing.

We forgive by questioning our beliefs or merely being present to them. We see that everyone is doing their best with the thinking they have in the moment. Out of this understanding, resentment can dissolve.

We can forgive ourselves in the same way, by seeing the truth of who we are – that we are not our opinions of ourselves.

We can be grateful that we have the freedom to be who we want to be, guided by inner wisdom, unshackled and unburdened, living life in a state of ease, wellness, and openness.

FINAL WORDS

"People say that what we're all seeking is a meaning for life... I think that what we're seeking is an experience of being alive, so that our life experiences on the purely physical plane will have resonances with our own innermost being and reality, so that we actually feel the rapture of being alive." — Joseph Campbell

We can see that, with the endowment of the incredible human gift of imagination and creative visualisation, it is easy to use thoughts in a way that does not serve us.

The three principles of Mind, Consciousness, and Thought – as described in simple terms by Syd Banks – show the building blocks that make up our experience.

Understanding how they interrelate is to receive the master key to a world of new possibilities. Having the opportunity to share them with you, brings me the same joy as did learning and performing magic tricks all those years ago.

One person's experience of life can be enormously more joyful than their neighbour's simply as a result of how they use the gift of thought. We don't need to learn how to control our thoughts; we need to stop letting them control us.

We can be either beholden to beliefs that create unnecessary suffering or choose to have our experience reflect continual peace. We all can enjoy the latter.

WHAT I HOPE THAT, from reading this, you have come to see the limitless potential that we all have when we realise that the only thing restricting mental freedom is our personal mind; the thinking that it stirs, and to which it clings.

For every belief that pulls us into the caverns of despair, we have the option of awakening from our dream by choosing peace.

We can navigate a continually-expanding and limitless reality.

When there is "burnout," I am one thought away from being a force of nature.

When I feel fear, I am one thought away from love.

When I fear losing money, I am one thought away from knowing that I can make more than I have ever imagined.

When others reject me, I am a thought away from a sense of total connection to all things.

When I'm in a bad mood, I am a thought away from excitement.

When my past defines me, I am one thought away from timeless presence.

. . .

THE MORE WE buy into the concept that we live in a solid, objective reality, which affects how we feel and behave, the more we suffer.

We are not at the mercy of things happening "out there," no matter how serious those things may seem. We can be okay, regardless of the circumstances.

> *"Limitation is always illusion. Just wait. Relax. Stay still. Wait until the wisdom talks to you, as it will."* — Sydney Banks

We think, but we are not the things that we believe we are.

We live in the experience of our thinking, and what we resist can feel solid. Instead of resisting, we need to learn to love what-is unconditionally, even though this isn't always easy at first.

When we are gentle with what is there, nothing is impossible. It becomes an opportunity to realise our innate wellness through the practice of non-resistance. Our reality becomes a beautiful game of transcending the ego and immersing ourselves in the golden glow of connectedness that unites all things.

REGULARLY ASK YOURSELF "WHO AM I?" and you will see that what you think you know about yourself is illusory.

There is undoubtedly something magnificent in the idea that we continually create our entire experience. There is magic in the understanding that we can create whatever we like, and that we can allow a force greater than ourselves to guide and heal us if we choose, to keep us energised, connected, and alive.

We can live creatively or see ourselves as victims of our

circumstances. Knowing this might change everything for you, as it has for me, because all it takes is choice.

And when you make the creative choice, all that remains is possibility.

THANK YOU FOR READING.

If you found this book helpful, I would be grateful for a review, which you can send to me directly at alex@alexmathers.net, or even better, do share it on Amazon or other platforms where this book is found.

ABOUT THE AUTHOR

Alex Mathers is a nomadic English/Austrian writer, coach and illustrator, born in Copenhagen in 1984. He spent his twenties building a global design business and consultancy. Now he mostly writes articles, stories and books, and helps others be better writers.

He loves monkeys, air-breathing, sea creatures, walking, science fiction and tea.

He supports people in creating their masterpiece, whether it be a dream book, a blog, or a creative project, and overcoming their limits.

He lives all over the world, depending on what adventure interests him next. He has lived in Japan, Georgia, Vietnam, Thailand, Jamaica and Barbados.

You can follow more of his work, books, newsletter, articles, classes, podcasts, and films via his personal site: www.alexmathers.net.

In fact, you should definitely follow his newsletter, because you will hear of new writing, bonuses, classes and books coming out from him there.

Contact Alex there if you would like to ask him a question, say hi, or inquire about personal coaching.

You can also connect with him and follow his work via the social media links below.

∼

facebook.com/iamalexmathers
twitter.com/iamalexmathers
instagram.com/alexjmathers
amazon.com/author/alexmathers

FURTHER RECOMMENDED READING

The following are great reads if you want to go further into the subjects discussed in this book:

'The Enlightened Gardener' — Sydney Banks

'Clarity: Clear Your Mind, Have More Time, Make Better Decisions and Achieve Bigger Results' — Jamie Smart

'Real: The Inside-Out Guide to Being Yourself' — Clare Dimond

'The Inside-Out Revolution: The Only Thing You Need to Know to Change Your Life Forever' — Michael Neill

'Somebody Should Have Told Us! Simple Truths for Living Well' — Jack Pransky

∽

FREE BONUS BOOK:

'The Five Secret Truths:

Uncover your confidence, work with your fear, and be unstoppable.'

Learn the 'Five Secret Truths' that helped Alex overcome anxiety, see hidden opportunities, tap into boundless creativity and energy, and create a tremendous 'unfair advantage' in his life.

Follow these steps right now to grab your free booklet copy before it's gone:

- Head to alexmathers.net/5stbook
- Sign up to Alex's newsletter
- Click the download link in your email for instant download of the book

If you are looking for a simple list of five powerful reminders to help you uncover your unstoppable energy, this is the book for you.

ALSO BY ALEX MATHERS

Promo 3.0

How to Get Illustration Clients

The Indispensable Illustrator

Joining the Dots

The Five Secret Truths